Behold

Mother Mary
Divine Mother of the Universe

Inspiration for the heart and soul

Robin D. Rose

Behold Mother Mary
Divine Mother of the Universe

All prayer, collected by, inspired or given to
Robin D. Rose

Copyright © 2011 Robin Rose

All rights reserved.

ISBN-13: 978-1519244925

ISBN-10: 1519244924

Published through Living Wisdom Press

DEDICATION

*"Dear children, I want to thank you for your sacrifice, and I invite to the greatest sacrifice, the **sacrifice of love**.*

Without love, you are not able to accept neither me nor my Son. Without love, you cannot witness your experiences to others. That is why I invite you dear children, to begin to live the love in your hearts."

Mother Mary, 3-27-1986 Medjugorje

FORWARD

Mother Mary is the ultimate symbol of the Divine Feminine and the symbol of Grace within the Soul. Through Divine Feminine Grace we receive and share this power of God's greatest gift, so that our hearts and minds are released from our ego's burdens. As the Soul grows, it is nurtured by the Divine Feminine. This is the Spirit of Truth, Wisdom, and Light and reveals the secrets of the universe to each of us. The Divine Mother also teaches us the power of faith. This faith teaches us that in Christ, all is ONE and that all our needs are taken care of if we surrender to love and let that love guide our path. The mission of the Divine Mother is to point the way to her child, the Christ, and the power of love that dwells within our own hearts and souls.

The prayers in this booklet are a combination of traditional prayers along with some newly inspired or channeled prayers. Some are giving praise to the Mother, others are instructions from her for accessing our higher good. Also, many of these prayers are to help us except who we are as God's Divine Children.

In May of 2009, Mother Mary made what appeared to be a simple comment to me, but after thinking about it for a moment the meaning changed for me.

"To My Son, To My Son, bring them back to Christ."

A Course in Miracles refers to God's children, us, as the "Sonship." When I do my prayers, this is the term I use to pray for everyone's healing. I pray that we remember who we are and that only love fills our hearts.

The Course also tells us we are Christ, "men no longer, but at one with God."

I feel Mary is asking that we, as the Sonship, lead each other back to the Spirit of Love. How? By forgiving each other (and ourselves), by asking Her and other Divine beings for help in times of trial and by extending Love (who we are) whenever possible.

The word "back" means a return — not something we have to attain or even earn but a simple return to who we have always been, but for now have forgotten. This concept can be summed up in one single sentence: "You are on a journey without distance to a place you never left." ACIM

Many blessings to you all.
Robin Rose

Prayer of Perfection

O Mary let thy eminent perfection draw forth the perfection from within me,

That I may stand in the Light of thy Son,

Let the purity of thy spirit come forth to water the earth and bring life to its children.
The Immaculate Heart Servants of Mary

Faith

The only thing that prevents your good from coming into natural and continuous expression is your lack of real faith and trust in the God within you-your, Christ self.
As Given to Joseph Benner-The Way Out 1916

Robin D. Rose

Mother

Mother, Guide all my endeavors as I call upon the endless love of God.

The Compassion Prayer

O Giver of All Life,
Help Me to See All Things healed
and at one as God has created them.

Help Me to remember My Divinity
with assistance from the Holy Spirit.
Guide my thoughts, words and deeds,
For the Betterment of All Beings,

Help Me to Grow in Love, Wisdom, and Compassion, to Heal Myself and the Children of Earth.
Help Me To Give of Myself Without Thought.
Help Me and All Beings to Fully Realize The Forgiveness and the Fullness Of the Love of God.

Help Me To Bring To the Children of Earth
An Understanding of the Way of Love.

Glory Unto all of God's Children,
Glory Unto the Christ. Glory Unto God.
And so it is.

Forgiveness and Love

Pray, pray, pray. Not to get, but to give. Pray for others knowing in your heart in doing so you pray for yourself. Your Heavenly Father knows what you need and will act accordingly to benefit his children.

Please remember that He knows what is best for you and the outcome may not look as you wanted it to but it will answer the prayer that is really in your heart.

The most needed prayers must be for forgiveness and love. They must be to heal that which is tearing you apart from your true desires, to love and to be loved.

Love not of a human or for a human but the pure love of God. The love that transcended the cross and showed the world we are not of it, but merely a guest in it. That love is called Christ. When your focus is on love and healing, whether you know it or not, everyone will step closer to the kingdom of Heaven.
The Divine Mother to Robin Rose

In the Name of the Father

I pray these things in the name of our Father:

I pray that Peace is in my heart now and always.

I pray that Peace fills my mind and

transforms my vision.

I pray that Forgiveness releases the past and sets me free

I pray that Forgiveness opens my heart and makes clear my vision for the future.

I pray that Love clears my mind and embraces my heart.

I pray that Love surrounds me and remains my focus now and forever. And so it is.

Mary's Grace

Hail Mary, one with Grace,
the Lord is with us through you.
Blessed are we by your miracle,
and by the miracle love of your son, Jesus.
Holy Mary, Mother of Miracles,
we surrender our fears, now and forever.

We accept God's unconditional love, and see the Miracle Kingdom manifest on Earth.

Letting Go

I have nothing new to say, nothing profound. I say today as I have said all along. Love, open your heart. Set yourself and your brothers free. Accept that you are Christ, all of you.
Pray for love to overtake you.
Pray to release your brothers from the prison you have condemned them to.
Pray that each day when you see those whom you hold a grievance that you can let them go.
Pray that on this day that they may be blessed.
Pray for the strength to love others you have judged as unworthy of your love.
Pray that you can see others as the

Heavenly Father sees them, as his holy children--whole and perfect in every way.
Divine Mother to Robin Rose

O Blessed Mother Immaculate

O Blessed Mother Immaculate
Mother of Our Lord, Christ Jesus,
Help Us to Come Closer to Thee
That We May More Fully Perceive Thee
That We May Better Know Thee
And Our Lord and Master Christ Jesus.
May We Be So Filled with Light
That Our Presence May Be Healing for the Sick,
And That Our Touch May Bring Wholeness To Those in Need.
Bring Our Consciousness to Ever See
The Perfection in All Things Created
By the One God of All.
Assist Us that We May Fully Realize
The Great Gift of Atonement,
And the Message Of Love, Wisdom, and Compassion

Given Unto Us by You and Your Son.
Bring Peace and Blessings to Us
And to Those Around Us,
And Grant to Us A Greater Realization
Of Ourselves
As Children of Light,
In Thy Name, Blessed Mother Mary
And In the Name of Our Lord Jesus
Christ.
Amen.

O Blessed Mother Mary Guide Us

O Blessed Mother Mary
Even as the Spirit of God
Does Guide and Watch over Us,
So Guide Thou also Me
Unto the Depths of My Own True Self.

Let the Purity of Thy Spirit Come Forth
To Water the Earth And Bring
Life to Its Children,
In the Spirit of Love, Wisdom,
and Compassion.

O Blessed Mother Mary,
May Thy Glory
Draw Forth the Glory from Within Me,
That I May Stand in the Light
of the Christ,
With the Joy of Knowing
That I Am One with Thee
And Our Lord Christ
In the Body of the Holy Assembly.

O Blessed Mother Mary,
Strengthen Our Hearts and Minds
With Divine Love, Wisdom,
and Compassion
That We May Better Serve With Thee,
And Christ.

Glory Unto all of God's Children.
Glory Unto the Christ. Glory Unto God.
And so it is.

Prayer for Today

Children pray daily recognizing that this is the only moment in which we are living:

Today I stand before you Lord, and I ask for you to be in my heart, my soul and my mind.

I surrender my thoughts of pain and anger to you.

I surrender to you all memories that keep my mind, body and soul from your peace.

I ask that you take all human misperception and turn it into God vision.

I ask that God's will be done through me and with the best of intentions.

I accept God's pure loving vision and

allow it to pour from my heart to all of whom I cross paths.

I accept God's vision as truth and feel honored to know his love is flowing from me.

I pray these things Oh Lord, in the name of our Holy Father. And so it is.

Forgiveness

By the grace of God I ask that forgiveness fill my heart.

I understand Lord, that the willingness to Forgive, is the first step to knowing mercy.

I ask that through my willingness to forgive Father, all are set free.

I acknowledge that through my willingness to forgive myself, I will know your wisdom.

With your wisdom Father, I understand

how Forgiveness leads to Love.

By the grace of the Mother and the guidance of the Holy Spirit, I accept forgiveness

And through that acceptance, we are released of from the bondage of the past

I surrender that past to the Holy Spirit and let it return into the nothingness from which it came.

Gratitude

Children, do you know the true power of Gratitude? The word of God tells us to give thanks to the Father for all. Not just what stands before us now, but for all that is to come. Giving thanks shows our Father you have faith, knowing that he will take care of you. That has always been his promise, and I am here to remind you of this.

I am grateful today in this moment for the gifts God has bestowed upon me.

I am grateful for your love Lord, for it sets me free

I am grateful for all whom I will meet this day as I will bless them as you have blessed me

I am grateful for every challenge that stands before me and for the victory of overcoming them

I am grateful that your wisdom fills me and sets me free from the consequences of my mistakes.

I am grateful that I learn from my mistakes and use those lessons to better myself and others.

I am grateful that each day in the faces of my brothers and sisters I see your face Lord.

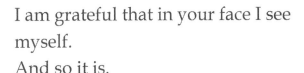

I am grateful that in your face I see myself.
And so it is.

God is Father and Mother

God is Father; God is Mother,
never one without the other.
Your balanced union is our source,
your Love will keep us on our course.
You offer us abundant life,
to free us from all sense of strife.
We plunge ourselves into the stream,
awakening from this bad dream.
We see that life is truly one,
and thus our victory is won.
We have returned unto our God,
on the path the saints have trod.
We form God's body on the Earth,
and give our planet its rebirth,
into a Golden Age of Love,
with ample blessings from Above.
We set all people free to see

that oneness is reality,
and in that oneness we will be
whole for all eternity.
And now the Earth is truly healed,
all life in God's perfection sealed.
God is Father, God is Mother,
we see God in each other.

Traditional Prayers

The following prayers come from around the world are consider traditional. For those who prefer the old world style these are the most popular and have provided comfort from many in times of trouble.

There is a part of me that loves the old style and I too have been in a place where their tradition brings me a foundation for my communion time.

Personal Requests

O Thou, by Whom we come to God, The Life, the Truth, the Way;
The path of prayer Thyself hast trod:
Lord, teach us how to pray! --James Montgomery, 1818

I have a mission... I am a link in a chain, a bond of connection between persons. God has not created me for naught... Therefore I will trust him.

Whatever, wherever I am, I can never be thrown away.
God does nothing in vain. He knows what he is about.
  J. H. Newman

Prayer to Our Lady of Mount Carmel

O Most beautiful flower of Mount Carmel, fruitful vine, splendor of Heaven, Blessed Mother of the Son of God, Immaculate Virgin, assist me in this my necessity. O Star of the Sea, help me and show me herein You are my Mother.

O Holy Mary, Mother of God, Queen of Heaven and Earth, I humbly beseech You from the bottom of my heart to succor me in this necessity. There are none that can withstand Your power.

O show me herein You are my Mother. O Mary conceived without sin, pray for us who have recourse to Thee. (Three times)

Sweet Mother, I place this cause in Your hands. (Three times) Amen

Traditional Hail Mary

Hail Mary full of grace the Lord is with thee,
Blessed are you among women,

Blessed is the fruit of thy womb Jesus ,

Holy Mary, Mother of God, pray for us now and at the hour of our deaths.

Prayer to Our Lady of Bistrica

Immaculate Mother of Jesus, We honor You as God's chosen one, beautiful, beloved, and free from all sin.

Keep watch over us, pray that we may rise above our sins and failings and come to share the fullness of grace.

Be a Mother to us in the order of grace by assisting us to live your obedience, your faith, your hope and your love. Amen

Prayer to Our Lady of Fatima

O Most Holy Virgin Mary, Queen of the most holy Rosary, you were pleased to appear to the children of Fatima and reveal a glorious message.

We implore you, inspire in our hearts a fervent love for the recitation of the Rosary.

By meditating on the mysteries of the redemption that are recalled therein may we obtain the graces and virtues that we ask, through the merits of Jesus Christ, our Lord and Redeemer. Amen

Prayer to Our Lady of Lourdes

O Immaculate Virgin Mary, Mother of Mercy, you are the refuge of sinners, the health of the sick, and the comfort of the afflicted.

You know my wants, my troubles, my sufferings.

By your appearance at the Grotto of Lourdes you made it a privileged sanctuary where your favors are given to people streaming to it from the whole world.

Over the years countless sufferers have obtained the cure for their infirmities -- whether of soul, mind, or body.

Therefore I come to you with limitless confidence to implore your motherly intercession.

Obtain, O loving Mother, the grant of my requests. Through gratitude for Your favors, I will endeavor to imitate

Your virtues that I may one day share in Your glory. Amen

Prayer to Our Lady, Help of Christians

Mary, powerful Virgin, You are the mighty and glorious protector of the Church.

You are the marvelous help of Christians.

You are awe inspiring as an army in battle array.

In the midst of our anguish, struggle, and distress, defend us from the power of the enemy, and at the hour of our death, receive our soul in Heaven. Amen

Prayer to Our Lady of Czestochowa (Our Lady of Perpetual Help)

O Mother of God, Immaculate Mary, to Thee do I dedicate my body and soul, all my prayers and deeds, my joys and sufferings, all that I am and all that I have.

With a joyful heart I surrender myself to Thy love.

To Thee will I devote my services of my own free will for the salvation of mankind and for the help of the Holy Church whose Mother Thou art.

From now on my only desire is to do all things with Thee, through Thee, and for Thee.

I know I can accomplish nothing by my own strength, whereas you can do everything that is the will of Thy Son, Our Lord Jesus Christ.

You are always victorious. Grant, therefore, O Helper of the Faithful, that my family, my parish, and my country might become in truth the Kingdom where Thou reigns in the glorious presence God the Father, God the Son, and God the Holy Spirit, forever and ever. Amen

The Magnificent (Canticle of Mary)

My soul proclaims the greatness
of the Lord,
my spirit rejoices in God my Savior;
for He has looked with
favor on His servant
From this day all generations
shall call me blessed.
The Almighty has done great things
for me, and holy is His Name
He has mercy on those who
follow Him in every generation.
He has shown the strength of His arm,
He has scattered the proud
in their conceit.
He has cast down the mighty
from their thrones,

and has lifted up his followers.
He has filled the hungry
with good things,
and the selfish He has sent away empty.
He has come to the help of His children
for He has remembered
His promise of mercy,
the promise He made to
our fathers, to Abraham and his
children forever.
Amen

Prayer to Our Lady of Guadalupe

Our Lady of Guadalupe, mystical rose, intercede for the Church, protect the Holy Father, and help all who invoke You in their necessities.

Since You are the ever Virgin Mary and Mother of the True God, obtain for us from Your Most Holy Son the grace of a firm and sure hope amid bitterness of life, as well as an ardent love and the precious gift of final perseverance.

Dearest Lady, fruitful Mother of Holiness, teach me Your ways of gentleness and strength.

Hear my prayer, offered with deep felt confidence to beg this favor ...(state your request here)

O Mary, conceived without sin, I come to your throne of grace to share the fervent devotion of your faithful Mexican children who call to Thee under the glorious title "Guadalupe" the Virgin who crushed the serpent.

Queen of Martyrs, who's Immaculate Heart was pierced by seven swords of grief, help me to walk valiantly amid the sharp thorns strewn across my path.

Invoke the Holy Spirit of Wisdom to fortify my will to frequent the Sacraments so that, thus enlightened and strengthened, I may prefer God to all creatures and shun every occasion of sin.

Help me, as a living branch of the Vine that is Jesus Christ, to exemplify His divine charity always seeking the good of others.

Queen of Apostles, aid me to win souls for the Sacred Heart of my Savior. Keep my apostolate fearless, dynamic, and articulate, to proclaim the loving solitude of Our Father in Heaven so that the wayward may heed His pleading and obtain pardon, through the merits of Your Merciful Son, Our Lord Jesus Christ. Amen

Mary, Queen of Missions

Holy Mary, Our Mother, today, each day and in our last hour, we entrust ourselves entirely to Your loving and singular care.

We place in Your hands our entire hope and happiness, our every anxiety and difficulty, our whole lives.

May our every endeavor be directed and guided according to the Will of Your Son, which is Your wish, by the aid of Your prayer and special favor with God. Amen

Prayer to Our Mother of Perpetual Help

O Mother of Perpetual Help, grant that I may ever invoke Thy most powerful name, which is the safeguard of the living and the salvation of the dying. O Purest Mary, O Sweetest Mary, let Your name henceforth be ever on my lips.

Delay not, O Blessed Lady, to help me whenever I call on You, for, in all my needs, in all my temptations, I shall never cease to call on You, ever repeating Your sacred name, Mary, Mary.

O what consolation, what sweetness, what confidence, what emotion fills my soul when I pronounce Your sacred name, or even only think of You! I thank God for having given You, for my good, so sweet, so powerful, so lovely a name.

But I will not be content with merely pronouncing Your name; let my love for You prompt me ever to hail You, Mother of Perpetual Help. Amen

Prayer

Prayer is the soul's sincere desire,

Unuttered or expressed;
The motion of a hidden fire
That trembles in the breast.

Prayer is the burden of a sigh,
The falling of a tear
The upward glancing of an eye,
When none but God is near.

Prayer is the simplest form of speech
That infant lips can try;

Prayer the sublimest strains that reach
The Majesty on high.

Prayer is the contrite sinner's voice,
Returning from his ways,
While angels in their songs rejoice
And cry, "Behold, he prays!"

Prayer is the soul's vital breath,
The soul's native air, Our watchword at
the gates of death;
We enter heaven with prayer.

The saints in prayer appear as one
In word and deed and mind,
While with the Father and the Son
Sweet fellowship they find.

Nor prayer is made by man alone,
The Holy Spirit pleads,
And Jesus on the eternal throne
For sinners intercedes.

O Lord

O Lord, we bring before you
the distress and dangers of peoples and nations,
the pleas of the imprisoned and the captive,
the need of the refugee,
the weariness of the despondent,
and the diminishment of the aging.

O Lord, stay close to them all.
Saint Anselm of Canterbury

Prayers for Today

Today is new, unlike any other day,
for God makes each day different.

Today God's everyday grace
falls on my soul like abundant seed,
though I may hardly see it.

Robin D. Rose

Today is one of those days
Jesus promised to be with me,
a companion on my journey,

And my life today, if I trust him,
has consequences unseen.
My life has a purpose.

2009 Mary's Rosary

The following Rosary was given to me so that I would continue to pray it and share it with others.

The Apostles Creed

I believe in God the Father, Creator of heaven and earth and in the Christ whom we are.

I believe in the death of the ego and the resurrection of spirit.

I believe in the Kingdom of God reigning in our hearts and directing our thoughts.

I believe in the Holy Spirit as a guide and communicator with the angels, saints and ascended masters whom willingly await our call. I believe as a

Christed being, I AM life everlasting.
Amen

Lord's Prayer

Our Father, who art in heaven, hallowed be thy name.
Thy Kingdom come, thy will be done, in earth as it is in heaven Give us this day our daily bread.
And forgive us our trespasses, as we forgive those who trespass against us.
And lead us not into temptation, but deliver us from evil.
For thine is the kingdom, the power and the glory, forever and ever. Amen

Hail Mary

Hail Mary full of grace the Lord is with thee.

Blessed are ye among women, blessed is

the fruit of thy womb Jesus.

Holy Mary, mother of God, pray for us now and forever. Amen

Glory Be

Glory be to the Father, his Son and the Holy Spirit for as we were in the beginning, we are now and ever shall be one in Christ. Amen

O My Jesus

O my Jesus, teach us to forgive that we may remember heaven and that we may revel heaven to those seeking your mercy. Amen

Holy Queen

Hail Holy Queen, Mother of us all, you bring mercy and hope to comfort our hearts.

To you we surrender our earthly plight and allow your loving grace to comfort us.

Holy Mother to you we surrender and give way to the love and blessings of your son the Christ. Amen

O God

O God, who's blessed us with eternal life through the path of surrender and resurrection, we pray upon the Holy rosary so that you may guide us in words and deeds.

We your children are blessed by the Holy Trinity with clarity, wisdom and divine presence.

We accept the gift of atonement shown us by our brother Jesus, who lived, died and was born again in our true identity, the Christ. Amen

Positive quotes to ponder on…

"What we are is God's gift to us. What we become is our gift to God."
Eleanor Powell

"Being happy doesn't mean that everything is perfect. It means that you've decided to look beyond the imperfections"

"Never mistake knowledge for wisdom. One helps you make a living; the other helps you make a life." Sandra Carey

Robin is a author, minister, and Truth teacher, whose love for God is evident in all her works. She is an artist and a Sacred Journey leader. Whatever Robin does, her intentions are to bring herself and other back to the truth that "we are now and always have been at one the Father."

Other Books by Robin D Rose:

Reaching For the Stars – Children's book

The Light Under the Door – Children's book

Mother Mary and the Undoing Process

Reflections of Truth

www.spiritualawakeningnow.com

www.universallightworkers.com

www.RobinRose.co